LEARNING FROM OUR LEADERS

THE STORY OF Sarah Schenirer

LEARNING FROM OUR LEADERS

THE STORY OF Sarah Schenirer

SARAH FELDBRAND
ILLUSTRATED BY RACHELI DAVID

I would like to express my thanks to the staff at Israel Bookshop for their superb work with this book. Thank you to the editor, Mrs. Malkie Gendelman; the proofreaders, Mrs. Faige Badian and Mrs. Rochelle Gemal; and the illustrator, Mrs. Racheli David.

ISBN 978-1-60091-536-9

Distributed by:
Israel Bookshop Publications
501 Prospect Street
Lakewood, NJ 08701
Tel: (732) 901-3009 / Fax: (732) 901-4012
www.israelbookshoppublications.com
info@israelbookshoppublications.com

Printed in the United States of America

Distributed in Israel by:
Shanky's
Petach Tikva 16
Jerusalem
972-2-538-6936

Distributed in Australia by:
Gold's Book and Gift Company
3-13 William Street
Balaclava 3183
613-9527-8775

Distributed in Europe by:
Lehmanns
Unit E Viking Industrial Park
Rolling Mill Road,
Jarrow, Tyne & Wear NE32 3DP
44-191-430-0333

Distributed in South Africa by:
Kollel Bookshop
Northfield Centre
17 Northfield Avenue
Glenhazel 2192
27-11-440-6679

CHAPTER ONE

The Seamstress from Cracow

Over 130 years ago, a little girl was born in Cracow, one of the largest cities in Poland. The little girl's name was Sarah Schenirer. In those days, Cracow—like most places—had no Jewish girls' schools. Girls had to go to the state school with the non-Jewish children until they were about twelve years old. But Sarah was lucky. Her parents were able to teach her everything a Jewish girl needs to know.

Sarah loved to learn, to *daven*, and to do mitzvos. Her father and mother were delighted with how good and how clever she was. They told her that she must try to do well at school, too, so she made sure to study hard. She actually enjoyed doing homework,

and her teacher would tell the other students, "Look at Sarah, and you will learn how to study."

As soon as Sarah learned to read the *aleph-beis*, the Yiddish books in the family bookcase became her best friends. When she wasn't in school or helping at home, she loved nothing better than to go off into a corner and read from *sefarim*. Her father, seeing how much she loved to learn, bought her a set of *Ein Yaakov*, so she could read about the stories in the Gemara. Her friends would say that when she was deep in her reading, thieves could empty the house of its contents and Sarah would never notice. She knew it was true. She especially loved the long winter Shabbos nights, when she had plenty of time to settle down with her beloved *sefarim*.

Her friends thought that Sarah was strange for spending so much time reading and thinking. "What are you thinking about?" Sarah's friend Mirele asked her one Shabbos afternoon, when a group of them was gathered at Mirele's house.

"I'm thinking about why people do things."

"What do you mean?" Mirele asked, surprised.

"Well," Sarah replied, "what makes a girl break a halachah, like braiding her hair on Shabbos, or eating something that may not really be kosher?"

Mirele shrugged. "What does it matter?" she said. "None of us worry about such old-fashioned laws from so long ago! We just like to think about pretty clothes and things like that. You really are such a '*frummie*'!" Mirele laughed, and the other girls laughed along with her.

Sarah knew that her friends were on the wrong track, but she did not know how to explain how right it felt to do what Hashem wanted of her. She thought, *I will learn and learn, and when I know enough, I will be able to explain to the others what being a Yid really means.* So, she studied and learned from her precious *sefarim* as much as she could.

When she was thirteen, Sarah left school and started to work so that she could help bring in some

much-needed money for her family. She became an expert seamstress, and she let her friends know that she was available to sew for them. As Sarah worked, she would say verses from Tehillim, just like the great Rebbe Reb Hirsch of Riminov, who also started out as a tailor, would do.

At first, the jobs Sarah did were small: Mrs. Hoenig wanted fuller sleeves; Mrs. Kusewitsky wanted more ruffles. Whatever Sarah did, she always did well and with her whole soul. She missed school, but she felt good being able to help out her family in whatever small way she could.

Most of her customers were demanding, but Sarah had endless patience, and she really tried to make every customer happy. Still, Sarah was a deep thinker. Just because she was no longer in school, it didn't stop her mind from whirring. No matter how tired she was at the end of the day, she would never go to sleep without reaching for one of her beloved *sefarim*. Those few minutes spent learning

gave her the strength to keep going. And during the day, while sewing for the ladies who insisted that the fit of their dress be just right, she had a lot to think about.

As she wrote in her diary, *These ladies want their clothes to be perfect. If only they cared as much about their* neshamos *being perfect…*

Sarah's customers were mainly *chassidishe* women and girls, like she herself was. But they did not share the standards of *tznius* that Sarah had. They would ask Sarah to shorten their sleeves or lower their neckline, according to the latest fashion trends.

Sarah couldn't help it. She might have only been hired to do a job, but she felt that she needed to say something to these women. In just the right way, she tried to explain to them that these fashions were not for a Jewish woman or girl, but more often than not, the customers did not listen to her.

This hurt Sarah very much. She would ask herself, *Isn't there anything that can be done to change things? How I wish I could convince these women to do the right thing!*

CHAPTER TWO

A Tragic Problem

Sarah's longing to do things right had her staying up late at night, working on the dresses she was sewing. Her mother couldn't help noticing that Sarah was always tired. Knowing how much her daughter loved the beauty of nature, she suggested that Sarah take a vacation with her friends.

Sarah knew how much the family needed the money she earned. How could she go away? So she hugged her mother and said, "Thank you for your offer, dear Mother, but times are too hard. Hashem will give me the strength I need without our having to spend money."

Her mother did not give up, though, and somehow she managed to convince Sarah to take a vacation.

Sarah decided to go with some friends to Zakopane, which was a beautiful town surrounded by the towering Tatra Mountains.

The trip there was exhausting, but Sarah was up bright and early the next morning. While her friends slept, she got right to work, happy with the unique mitzvah opportunity that was hers. With a smile at the thought of her friends' pleased reaction, she heated the stove to warm the room, bought fresh rolls, and prepared a hot breakfast.

The others woke up to a toasty, warm room. The table was beautifully set with food and drinks, all ready for them.

"Sarah, you were as tired as we were!" Gittel exclaimed. "You deserved to sleep late, too."

"Tomorrow, *I* will be the one to get the stove going and prepare breakfast," Leah announced with determination. Sarah simply smiled. She wasn't ready to give up her special mitzvah, but was wise enough to know that arguing was unnecessary.

The girls couldn't get enough of the refreshing, crisp air. They hired a carriage to take them up to the first stop on the mountain. From there, they rented sleds to slide down the snowy hill. Up with the carriage and down with the sled they went, again and again, for as long as their activity was accompanied by the sun's warm rays.

The next day Leah got up extra early, intending to prepare breakfast for everyone else—but it was not to be. Sarah, you see, had awoken even earlier and was already putting the finishing touches on the breakfast.

Leah threw her head back and laughed. "I should have known you would never give up the opportunity to do a *chessed* for others."

Sarah's friends couldn't help but enjoy doing things with her. She had such wonderful *middos* and was a real pleasure to be around. Sarah also had a good sense of humor, and she liked stories, jokes, and riddles. However, there was one thing

Sarah's friends didn't like about her, and that was what they called her "old-fashioned ideas." They had tried their best to convince Sarah to drop these ideas and do things like them, but Sarah was stubborn and would not change her ways. The girls had long ago decided to accept Sarah the way she was—they knew it was either that or they would lose out on the beautiful friendship they shared with her.

As Sarah gazed at the breathtaking scenery spread out before her, her heart nearly burst with her love and appreciation of Hashem. It was so easy to see Hashem's hand here, in these magnificent surroundings. She found herself saying one *pasuk* after another from Tehillim.

Seeing Sarah's reaction, the girls had an idea.

Giggling, Fradel called out, "Earth to Sarah! Sarah, come back!"

When Sarah didn't respond, the game was on, as each girl tried her best to get Sarah's attention. It was only when Rivkah threw a snowball at her back that Sarah finally looked up.

"Don't be such a *frummie*, Sarah!" Gittel chided even as she helped wipe the snow off Sarah's coat. "We are here to have a good time, not to say Tehillim. Leave that to your *bubby* back at home."

Sarah remained silent, but deep down, she was heartbroken. As she tried to join her friends in their fun, she couldn't help but wonder: *How could it be that they just didn't see what she saw, that they didn't feel what she felt, in a place like this, where Hashem's magnificence was present everywhere she turned?*

Sarah returned home refreshed but even more thoughtful than before.

• • •

One Friday night, Sarah's cousin Leah came to visit.

"Come with me, Sarah," she said. "There's a gathering for girls after the *seudah*. We need to hurry if we are going to make it there on time."

"Who will be there?" Sarah asked, unwilling to give up her Friday night learning for just any gathering.

"Girls and neighbors who you know well."

"Well...I suppose that will be good," Sarah answered, placing her finger in her beloved *sefer* as a placeholder until she could find something more permanent.

When they arrived, and Sarah saw the type of crowd that had already gathered, she once again asked Leah, "Are you sure this is the kind of place where a Jewish girl should be?"

Leah did not answer. She knew her old-fashioned cousin well and understood what would happen if she told her the truth, so she merely shushed Sarah as she pulled her inside.

"The speakers are about to begin!"

As they entered the room, Sarah could not believe her eyes. A young man without a yarmulke stood up at the front of the room. When he began to speak,

Sarah wanted to jump up and run away, but she couldn't. She had taken a seat with her cousin in the middle of the room, and climbing back out to the aisle to leave would have called way too much attention to herself.

She listened to the speaker and was horrified at the nonsense he was saying. It was pure *kefirah*! She couldn't believe her friends and neighbors, even more so her cousin who had brought her there, could really be taking this man's words seriously! Suddenly, a gas lamp went out. One of the girls who seemed to be in charge of the gathering got up and re-lit it.

Sarah felt the room begin to spin around her. The *chillul Shabbos* was just too much. "I've had enough," she said. Grabbing hold of Leah's hand, she pulled her cousin to her feet. "We're leaving," she told her, just as insistent as Leah had been when she'd told Sarah to come. Sarah too did not take no for an answer, and she half-led, half-dragged her cousin through the crowd and toward the door.

Once they were outside, Sarah turned on her. "How could this be happening?" she demanded. "How could their parents allow them to go to such a place? If these girls were ill, their parents would do whatever was needed to be done to help them get well. Why aren't the parents doing anything when their daughters' *neshamos* are dying?!"

Leah was still upset at being forced to leave, but in her heart, she knew Sarah was right. Seeing how distressed Sarah was now, she felt guilty for having forced her to come in the first place. She had only hoped to open her cousin's eyes to the possibilities of what was out there in the world, but it seemed Sarah would always be the same Sarah, stuck in her old-fashioned ways.

"Look, Sarah, that's just the way it is these days. What are you going to do about it?" she asked as they walked home. "Are you going to change the world? I don't think so, and that's why I brought you there—to show you what you're up against. Come

on, Sarah. Give it up already. It can't be you against the whole world, you know."

Sarah smiled. "Why not?" she replied. Then, slowing down, she said thoughtfully, "I know what needs to be done! We need schools...schools that will teach girls about *Yiddishkeit*."

"Jewish schools? For girls?!" Leah laughed out loud. "There is no such thing. You know that. Girls learn about *Yiddishkeit* from their mothers, at home...like you did and like I did."

"That's how it's been until now," Sarah agreed. "But Leah—it's not working anymore. Girls are being taught non-Jewish ways in the state schools... they're studying non-Jewish stories, poems, and songs—and it's causing the girls to become lost to *Yiddishkeit*! No! We need schools of our own. That will help save our girls!"

"And who's going to create these schools?" Leah asked, rolling her eyes at her silly cousin who would not listen to the voice of reason. "Will it be you?"

"Maybe it will," Sarah declared. "Maybe it will."

CHAPTER THREE

Sarah Schenirer's Dream

From the moment the idea of a Jewish school for girls entered Sarah's mind, it took hold of her entire life. The more Sarah looked around, the more she began to see young girls who were bored and uninspired, completely lacking an appreciation for the beauty of Torah and mitzvos. It pained Sarah so much to see Jewish homes falling apart, as one by one these girls left *Yiddishkeit*, seeking inspiration elsewhere. Only her diary knew just how sad she was. It was there that she confided all the details of her sorrow, as well as her dreams for what she wished to do to fix the current situation.

I want to bring back Jewish girls' pride in being the daughters of Hashem, she wrote in her diary.

I want to bring them to a place where they will be happy to fulfill Hashem's commandments.

Once she had an outline of how her school would work, she began thinking of how she could fill in the gaps. She knew her plans would take much time and effort to become reality, but of one thing she was sure: somehow, she would find a way to pass on to others the inspiration that she herself felt. She would do it.

Then, in the fall of 1914, World War I broke out. Immediately all of Sarah's plans and ideas were put on hold.

It wasn't long before Cracow became filled with the horrors of war. Each day brought new explosions, the whistling and whining of bombs falling, and the screams of the terrified townspeople. Sarah's family decided that they would be safer in Vienna, Austria, and so they planned to move.

Many others had the same idea as the Schenirer family. In fact, there were so many refugees

crowding into Vienna that for weeks, the Schenirers literally lived on the streets; there was simply no available house for them! Finally, they found a tiny apartment in a non-Jewish neighborhood.

The first question Sarah Schenirer asked their Jewish landlady was, "How far is it to the Jewish section of the city?"

"Oh, about an hour's walk."

"An hour! Oh, my!" Sarah's shoulders drooped. "I have always gone to shul on Shabbos. But an hour each way... " Her voice trailed off.

"Oh, you don't have to walk to the Jewish section to *daven*," the landlady told her. "There's a *frum* shul right around the corner—the Shtumper Street Shul."

When Sarah checked out this shul, she couldn't believe her eyes. This was a real shul, with serious *daveners*! On Shabbos the *rav*, Rav Moshe Flesch, would often speak. Rav Flesch had been a student of Harav Shamshon Raphael Hirsch, and he would speak about Rav Hirsch's teachings. These ideas

were new to Sarah—and very inspiring. She made sure to come to shul each Shabbos, where she would listen to Rav Flesch speak.

It was Shabbos Chanukah. Rav Flesch was speaking about the *Chashmona'im*. Sitting in shul, Sarah leaned forward to better hear the *rav's* words. Rav Flesch told the story of Chanah and her seven sons, he spoke about Chanah's greatness, as well as the greatness of every Jewish woman.

"That is why it is so important to teach girls—so that they will grow in their love for Torah," Rav Flesch said.

Sarah Schenirer was fascinated. She had often thought about such things but had never heard them explained as clearly as Rav Flesch was saying them now.

If only all my friends back in Cracow could be hearing this, too! she thought, ever faithful to her friends. *They could receive so much* chizuk *from the Rav's powerful words!*

Even while in Vienna, Sarah continued sewing to help support the family. All week long, as she sewed, she had time to think. One day, while making neat, even stitches on a dress sleeve, the thought occurred to Sarah: *Why don't I write down whatever I hear from the Rav? Then I can bring his words back to the girls of Cracow. I could give the girls* chizuk *like that!*

With this in mind, Sarah began to attend every class the Rav gave. She wanted to learn as much as she could. He taught Chumash, Tehillim, and *Pirkei Avos*, all in a way that young people would appreciate. Sarah paid close attention to each word he said, and in the evening, after her workday was over, she sat and wrote down everything. Her notes grew and grew.

Once, Sarah was in middle of sewing a billowy skirt. She tried to thread her needle—but she couldn't. She tried again and again, but she did not succeed. This had never happened to her. Suddenly, Sarah looked at the clock. She couldn't believe it:

the Rav would be starting his class right now! She had lost track of the time. She jumped up and raced out of the house and over to the shul, grateful that Hashem had sent her a reminder about the *shiur*.

Finally, at long last, the Schenirer family was ready to return to Cracow. Sarah carefully packed her precious notes, already planning how she would teach the girls of Cracow all the wonderful things she had learned.

But deep down, she worried: *Will the girls be interested in what I have to say?* Oh, how she hoped they would be! So much depended on it! She would find a way to teach them all she had learned so that they, too, would love Torah and mitzvos.

The clickety-clack of the train taking her back to Cracow seemed to echo her thoughts.

You will succeed! it seemed to chant. *You will succeed...you will succeed...*

CHAPTER FOUR

A Failed Attempt

Immediately upon arriving back in Cracow, Sarah Schenirer got to work. First she gathered a group of *frum* women so she could tell them about her plans. She began by describing the terrible situation.

"You are mothers of girls my age. You know better than anyone the tragedy that has happened to our girls!" she cried out. "They are like poor, lost sheep that have wandered into other fields and have not returned! They spend their time studying things that are not Jewish. If they don't know anything about *Yiddishkeit*, how can we expect them to stay Jewish?"

There was quiet in the room. Here and there, women were weeping. Many mothers had already lost their daughters to the modern ways.

After a moment's pause, Sarah Schenirer went on. "Crying is not enough," she told them gently. "We must do something about this."

"But what?" the women asked. "That's just the way it is today. What can we possibly do to change things?"

"We must give our daughters a Jewish education and a love of Jewish ideas. That is the only way."

There was silence. Then one of the women said disapprovingly, "Jewish education? But...learning is for boys! Girls should be at home, helping their mothers. Jewish girls have always remained at home."

Sarah Schenirer nodded. "Yes, girls should be at home...but *are* our girls at home? No. They are going to the non-Jewish schools. They study stories written by Polish authors. They sing songs in the Austrian-German language—"

Mrs. Schwartz rose to her feet. "You are so right!" she declared. "My daughter Sima is interested only

in non-Jewish subjects. Even after school is over for the day, she goes to meet with the other girls in her class—the Jewish ones and the non-Jewish ones... They speak Polish. They're ashamed when I speak Yiddish."

"Yes, and at night, they want to go to the theater to see non-Jewish plays," Mrs. Barsky added, sadly shaking her head.

Sarah Schenirer sighed. "You know, not very long ago, Jewish girls were not allowed in non-Jewish schools. But now the laws have changed..."

Mrs. Fried called out bitterly from the other side of the room, "How do you think you can persuade our girls to leave their Polish friends and to stop going to the theater and to non-Jewish gatherings?"

The other mothers agreed. "You don't need to persuade *us*. Our *daughters* are the ones you must convince!"

Sarah Schenirer realized that they were right. And so, with their help, she arranged for a gathering of their daughters.

The girls came because their mothers told them that a learned woman from Vienna was going to give a talk. Vienna was one of the most modern places of all, so the girls were very curious to hear what this woman had to say.

Sarah Schenirer began. "I'm sure you know, girls, that the Jewish custom is to read *Pirkei Avos* in the summer. But do you know why that is?"

The girls looked at each other. What was this? A lecture on *Yiddishkeit*? They began to squirm in their seats. The squirming soon turned into whispering and smirks, and then girls started leaving. One by one they walked out of the room. Their voices carried back to Sarah Schenirer. "What a fanatic! Where did she get those crazy ideas? Who wants to hear this?"

Sarah Schenirer felt very sad and broken. She had failed completely. All her dreams of inspiring the girls of Cracow had come to nothing. She made her way home and spent the evening crying to Hashem to help her find a way to reach the girls.

Racheli David

But while she might have failed this time, she refused to give up. If she gave up, what would become of the girls? How would they ever have the strength to build Jewish homes? How would they be able to stand up to whatever tests they might have to face in the years ahead? So she *davened* with all her heart, and she trusted that Hashem would help her and show her what to do next.

CHAPTER FIVE

With a Blessing from the Rebbe

As she struggled to find a way to interest the girls in learning, Sarah Schenirer did two things. First, she started a Jewish library, so that others who loved to read would be able to learn from Jewish books and *sefarim*, too. Quickly and quietly, as was her way, Sarah began her library. She collected *sefarim* from wherever she could find them. Her library shelves included the writings of Rav Hirsch, Rav Lehman, Rav Ehrman, and others.

The second thing she did was begin an after-school group for the few girls who were willing to come. After her long day of sewing, she would teach Torah to the girls in the group. Slowly, the group

grew. But every night, as she lay in bed, Sarah *davened* to be shown how she might reach even more girls.

Then one night, the answer came to her in a flash: *The little ones! We should start with them!*

Sarah was excited with the idea. *I'll get a group of young girls, and I'll teach them the* aleph-beis, she decided. *Their hearts have not yet been influenced by non-Jewish ideas. Then, as each grade grows older, a school will grow!*

The idea of starting a school for the girls of Cracow seemed so right to Sarah Schenirer. She wrote a letter to her brother in Czechoslovakia, asking for advice on how to get started. At first he argued with her, but when he saw that she would not give up, he wrote back, *My suggestion is that you come meet with the Belzer Rebbe. He is in Marienbad now. He will advise you on what to do.*

Sarah counted the money she had saved up. It wasn't much, but she had just enough for a trip

by carriage to Marienbad. Immediately she made plans to travel there so she could meet with the Rebbe, Rav Yissachar Dov of Belz.

It was a long and tiring journey, but as soon as she arrived, Sarah and her brother hurried straight to the Rebbe. Her brother wrote out a *kvittel* with their names. He added the words, "My sister wants to educate Jewish girls in the way of *Yiddishkeit* and Torah."

Soon it was their turn to go into the Rebbe. The Rebbe sat at the other side of the table. Sarah Schenirer had never seen such an angelic-looking person before. He looked like she imagined Avraham, Yitzchak, and Yaakov to have looked. The Rebbe read what was written on the *kvittel* and then said, "Surely you know that such is not our way..."

Sarah Schenirer took a deep breath. "Yes. But now things must change. It is the only way to save our daughters."

The Rebbe smiled. "*Nu, nu.* If that is the case, then *brachah v'hatzlachah*!"

JEWISH GIRLS' SCHOOL

Those words were like music to Sarah Schenirer's ears: *May you be blessed and may you succeed!* All the way back to Cracow, the Rebbe's blessing warmed her. It was still warming her as she tried to figure out a way to get started on her plans.

One morning, she had an idea. Reaching for a piece of paper, she wrote in large letters: "The seamstress Sarah Schenirer is available to sew children's clothing." She stuck the paper onto her door, kept her prices down, and soon she was flooded with customers. The mothers would bring their children with them so that the children could try on the new clothes that Sarah was sewing for them.

Sarah Schenirer was so kind and gentle that often the children stayed even after their fittings were over. When her room was full of little girls, Sarah would turn to them and ask, "Do you know what holiday is coming soon? Do you know why we celebrate Chanukah? Does anyone know who

Yehudis was?" She would offer prizes for the right answers, but the girls were silent.

"How would they know?" one of the mothers asked. "After all, they go to a non-Jewish school. They aren't taught such things!"

"That's true," Sarah Schenirer agreed. "But don't you think they *should* know?" Then, without waiting for the mother's reply, she turned to the children. "Dear girls, why don't you come back on Sunday? I will tell you the story of Chanukah. I will make you a cake and latkes, and we will talk about the mighty Yehudah and the brave Yehudis."

On Sunday the girls came back. Sarah Schenirer knew how to tell good stories. She added drama, putting life into every story she told. The mothers crowded into the hallway so that they, too, could hear Sarah's stories.

Word spread quickly among the mothers. The seamstress from Vienna knew so much! And she had such a good way of explaining things to young

children! It was true that none of them, or their mothers, had ever attended a Jewish school—but the Belzer Rebbe had blessed Sarah Schenirer with success, so her idea had to be good...

Still, most mothers were hesitant to be the first to enroll their daughters in a formal Jewish school, like Sarah Schenirer wanted to have. But Hashem sent Sarah Schenirer two people to help with the difficult beginnings. Her close friend Rebbetzin Halberstam, a granddaughter of the Divrei Chaim of Sanz, worked tirelessly to convince parents to send their children to Sarah's school, and Mr. Mordechai Luxenberg, a father who realized the importance of educating girls, sent two of his own daughters to her.

Sarah had just a few students enrolled, but it was enough. Her long-dreamed-of school was ready to be born.

On the 19th of Cheshvan, 1918, Sarah Schenirer wrote in her diary: *I have finally reached my goal. Today I began teaching Jewish girls in my very own*

school. Who can understand how exultant I feel? Until now, I have designed dresses for their bodies. Now I am creating clothing for their souls.

CHAPTER SIX

Bais Yaakov Begins

The very next morning, Sarah Schenirer changed the sign on her door. It now read simply: "School." She took the sewing machine, sewing table, and mirrors out of the room. In their place, she put a table and some chairs. There was no teacher's desk and no blackboard, but that didn't matter. Soon enough Sarah Schenirer's great and absorbing love for her young students, along with her ability to satisfy their thirst for stories and knowledge, had happy little girls coming day after day for more.

Sarah Schenirer's enormous energy was amazing. Her mind was full of ideas, and her heart beat a constant rhythm of so many hopes. She stayed up

late each night preparing the lessons for the next day. The girls really enjoyed the stories, but it was so difficult to get them to keep the mitzvos properly, because their older sisters or friends made fun of them for it.

When things were difficult, Sarah didn't stay sad for long. She just *davened* even harder, and oftentimes Hashem would reward her with a flash of inspiration that would leave behind a new idea to try.

Finally, after many years of hard work, Sarah began seeing results. The very young and pure girls she taught really wanted to learn and grow. And... more children wanted to join her school!

Soon Sarah had gathered twenty-five eager little girls in her class. The school became so big that girls had to sit on the floor and write on their laps—there simply was no more room around the table.

Outsiders continued to shake their heads and make fun of the school. Who could blame them?

After all, it was a school started by a seamstress. But the parents who entrusted their children to Sarah Schenirer, or Frau (Mrs.) Schenirer, as she was now called, saw a new spirit in their daughters' hearts.

"Do you know what happened yesterday?" one mother reported to Frau Schenirer. "When Rivkele saw her little brother drinking without saying a *brachah*, she cried out, 'Ahrele! You're a thief! Anyone who drinks Hashem's water without saying a *brachah* is like a thief! That's what Frau Schenirer taught us.' As I watched Ahrele saying a *brachah* out loud, I blessed you, Frau Schenirer, from the bottom of my heart!"

When she heard positive reports like this about her girls, Sarah Schenirer could only cry tears of joy. Her students spoke differently from the students of the Polish schools. They did not answer in Polish when spoken to in Yiddish. They did not answer with chutzpah. They showed respect to their parents. They wanted so much to go to shul and *daven*. They

enjoyed hearing stories about tzaddikim. They loved listening to their grandmothers reading *Tz'enah Ur'enah*. They were growing into true *bnos Yisrael*.

• • •

Sarah Schenirer was always coming up with ideas to make the girls feel privileged to be studying Torah. One day she walked into the classroom, barely able to control her excitement. She was holding a beautifully wrapped package in her hands.

"I have a gift for each one of you," she said. "I hope that you will like my present."

The girls crowded around their teacher, eager to see what the present was. She opened the package and pulled out a crisp white collar. She placed the collar around the neck of one of the girls and secured it with a button she had sewn on for that purpose. She did the same for each of the girls until they were all wearing beautiful white collars. The girls loved the present. They turned this way and that,

admiring what they could see of their own collars as well as the collars that adorned their friends. They felt beautiful and special, even without being told the meaning behind their new present.

"This is our school's new uniform," Frau Schenirer explained as she handed out the last one. "Be proud of it."

• • •

Sarah Schenirer herself dressed simply. She always wore dark clothing and dark stockings. Her brightest ornament was her warm smile. She began each day with the same words: "*Meidelach*, remember, you always stand before the *Heilige Bashefer*, the Holy Creator. He sees everything you do, hears everything you say, and writes down everything in a book."

Her messages might have been basic, but they were easy to remember, and the power of her faith and *yiras Shamayim* impressed her words

on the blackboards of the girls' minds. She was the living example of everything she wanted to teach her students.

Frau Schenirer knew that there were many ways to help a girl learn and grow. She made sure that the school day included all kinds of activities that her students would look forward to. Frau Schenirer enjoyed a good drama or musical. On Chanukah the girls put on a play that she had written in rhyme about Chanah and her seven sons. Sarah Schenirer had sewn the costumes herself, *davening* with each stitch that the play's message of complete devotion to Hashem would reach the hearts of those who were watching it. When the last curtain fell, there was silence as women wiped the tears from their eyes. For a long time, people couldn't stop talking about the wonderful performance.

For Tu B'Shevat, Sarah Schenirer wrote another play. Each of the students was a tree, all of them wishing that their wood would supply something of

value to the king. One tree said that it would like to give its wood for the king's scepter. Another wanted its wood to be used for the king's throne. A third hoped that its wood would be used for the steps up to the throne. Yet another tree dreamed of being the floor of the royal ballroom. One after another, the girls came forward and sang their parts. Then it was Raizel's turn to step forward and sing the finale:

"And me? A bench in Bais Yaakov is what I want to be.

"So that *Yiddishe kinder* will have where to rest,

"When they learn the Torah, which we love best!"

The mothers couldn't agree more. It was easy to tell by the thunderous applause.

• • •

One day, Sarah Schenirer had an important visitor, an honored member of the Cracow community. After watching her in action, he needed to understand more.

"What are you trying to do here?" he asked Frau Schenirer, when school was over for the day.

"I am trying to teach girls who will become the future wives and mothers of the Jewish People," Frau Schenirer replied, her eyes sparkling. "I want to make their *emunah* strong and to teach them our history, so that they will be proud to be Jewish instead of ashamed. I want them to understand how precious Jewish girls are."

The man was very impressed by Sarah Schenirer's words, her faith, and her burning desire to reach out to Jewish girls. But when he looked around again at the peeling paint, the worn table, and the half-broken chairs in the room, he sighed and said, "A school that is ensuring the future of the Jewish People—is this the way it should look?"

"Maybe not," Sarah Schenirer said, unbothered by his pointed words. "But what really counts is the joy that these girls are feeling about what they're learning here.

"You know," she continued, "we have twenty-five students learning here. Twenty-five is a very meaningful number. In *Lashon Hakodesh*, it's *chof hei*, which spells '*koh*.' Certainly, it's no coincidence that '*koh*' is the first word of Hashem's command to Moshe Rabbeinu at Har Sinai, regarding teaching Torah to the Jewish women."

The man nodded. He murmured the words from *Parshas Yisro* (*Shemos* 19:3) to which Frau Schenirer was referring: "*Koh somar l'Bais Yaakov*... So shall you say to the House of Yaakov [the women]..." Then he said, "I am the head of Agudas Yisrael in Cracow. I promise you that the Agudah will soon move your wonderful school into a big, beautiful building."

It took years of hard work until he was able to keep his promise and purchase such a big, beautiful building for Frau Schenirer's school. In the meantime, the Agudah arranged for Frau Schenirer and her students to move out of their original room and into an apartment on Katarzina Street.

Outside, there hung a large sign which read: *Bais Yaakov School for Girls*. That was the name that had been decided on for the school after the few words Sarah Schenirer had exchanged with the Agudah representative.

The old apartment building was on a run-down street. The steps leading up to the Bais Yaakov's apartment were in need of repair. The apartment itself consisted of exactly two rooms. The first room was a kitchen in which the girls took turns cooking. It was small and narrow and separated from the other room by a curtain. The second room was the classroom, in addition to serving as the dining room and sleeping quarters for the out-of-town girls.

Because there weren't enough chairs in the classroom, many of the girls sat on crates. (There were already forty students by the time they moved into this apartment.) The out-of-town girls who lived there slept two to a bed, on straw mattresses on the floor. Some nights it was so cold that it was hard

to fall asleep. Food wasn't plentiful either; dinner was often only kasha and a glass of milk. Many of the students came from well-to-do homes and were used to luxury, but still no one complained. The students were just so happy and eager to learn. They were Sarah Schenirer's students, after all, and everyone had always enjoyed being close with Sarah Schenirer.

When the Agudah stepped in, they took over all responsibilities for the school, leaving Sarah Schenirer in charge of only the teaching. It was a tremendous relief for her. Instead of being busy with fundraising and other technicalities, she could now put all of her energy into teaching her students—and that is what she did. She made every subject so interesting that the girls loved what they were studying, and they learned quickly.

CHAPTER SEVEN

Bais Yaakov's Success

Sarah Schenirer understood that so many had left *Yiddishkeit* because the beauty of the Torah had passed them by. People needed to be shown how special and wonderful it is to be a *frum* Jew. For this reason, Frau Schenirer did everything she could to fill the girls' days with enjoyment. The words "*Ivdu es Hashem b'simchah*—serve Hashem with joy" were always on her lips.

The girls' spiritual growth was always on Sarah Schenirer's mind. With love and warmth, she made sure that they mastered all the laws a Jewish girl must know. She inspired her students to love Hashem, Who created this beautiful world and gave

it to mankind to use and enjoy, and she taught the girls all about *tznius*, good *middos*, kindness, and so much more.

She tried very hard to help the girls develop closeness to one another. Whenever one of them was sick, Sarah Schenirer and the other girls would *daven* and say Tehillim for her. Frau Schenirer explained that their prayers, and especially their tears, had a tremendous impact up in Shamayim.

Frau Schenirer never needed to discipline her girls. The hurt in her eyes when a girl did something wrong, was usually enough to make the girl feel sorry. The girls loved Frau Schenirer too much to intentionally hurt her; they wanted only to make her happy.

If Frau Schenirer overheard a student speaking disrespectfully to another, or calling someone an insulting name, she would say, "I didn't expect to hear that from one of my Bais Yaakov girls," with a pained expression. The girl's face would fall and she

would instantly apologize, promising to try never to do it again. Frau Schenirer would smile and say, "I am sure that you will keep your word."

She didn't have to teach the girls about patience and self-control, they learned by her example. One cold morning, the girls overslept. Springing out of bed, they hurriedly put away their bedding. In her rush to get ready, one girl accidentally broke the expensive glass door. All of the girls feared Frau Schenirer's reaction. But when she heard of the accident, their beloved teacher had just one question: "Was anyone hurt?" Upon hearing that no one was injured, she sighed and said, "*Baruch Hashem*." Then, without another word, she calmly proceeded to sweep away the fragments of glass.

Sarah Schenirer saw her girls growing into young women with good, strong Jewish principles, and this made her very happy.

Sarah Schenirer and her Bais Yaakov movement literally changed the Jewish world. Instead of

wanting to fit in with the non-Jewish society, Jewish girls now began to feel fortunate and happy with their *Yiddishkeit*. They threw away their Polish novels and turned their attention to joyously studying a *pasuk* from *Navi* or a page from a *sefer*. Jewish practices and *minhagim* became precious to them. Girls stopped being ashamed of their parents' Yiddish, and began to speak it once again at home and in the streets, without fear of being called "old-fashioned." Once again girls took pride in the fact that their fathers and brothers learned Torah and that their mothers covered their hair. Once again having a Torah-centered home became the most important thing in these girls' lives.

CHAPTER EIGHT

Frau Schenirer: A True Baalas Chessed

The Jews of Cracow came to admire Sarah Schenirer. In addition to running her Bais Yaakov, she was always helping those in need. People streamed to her door, sometimes needing money, other times seeking encouragement. Sarah Schenirer made herself available to everyone. When it came to helping out the poor, including her students whose parents couldn't afford to pay for tuition, she would go from door to door, to homes and stores along Cracow's narrow streets, to collect money for them.

Most people gave generously. They knew that she lived only to help others, so how could they

refuse? Some only gave her a few *groschen* (a very small amount). Her friend who often accompanied her on these missions begged her not to visit the places that only gave her *groschen*. "Your time is too valuable," she said.

Sarah Schenirer shook her head. "True, I only get a few cents, but three people benefit from a donation: the person who gives it, the poor person who receives it, and myself. How can I deny these donors their profit, even if they only give such a small amount?" And she gave the same warm smile and blessing to those who gave a little as to those who gave a lot.

If Sarah Schenirer needed help with her *tzedakah* collections, her students would close their books and fan out to different homes to help her collect. Each Thursday, groups of girls would secretly distribute the *tzedakah* money to the needy people.

• • •

One day, right before Yom Tov, Sarah Schenirer found out about a young father who had no money at all. What did she do? She asked Reb Binyamin Zussman, an *askan* who would frequently help her with her missions, to slip a wad of cash into the young man's coat pocket when they were together in shul. Like this, the man would not be embarrassed. When the young father found the money, his joy was very great—but perhaps not nearly as great as that of Frau Schenirer, who was behind the whole act.

• • •

A sick boy, whose family did not have money, was in need of a serious operation in Vienna. It took Sarah Schenirer weeks to collect the funds to cover the cost. Her girls did what they could to help out, and they shared her joy when the mission was accomplished and the boy was sent off for his surgery. Then Sarah and her students completed their task by *davening* for the boy's speedy recovery.

• • •

Another time, Sarah Schenirer found out about a man whose *tallis* was so old and torn that he couldn't use it anymore. By the next day, she saw to it that he had a new *tallis*. The list of people she helped grew longer and longer. People noticed that the more she did, the more she seemed able to do.

• • •

One day Sarah Schenirer had just washed for *Hamotzi* when two women knocked on her door, asking for help. It was two o'clock in the afternoon, but Sarah had still not had a spare moment to eat the egg and hot cereal that her mother had prepared for breakfast.

Sarah's elderly mother saw the untouched plate of food and sighed. "They don't let you live," she said. "You haven't had a thing to eat or drink all day. You'll get so weak. Where will all this end?"

Sarah Schenirer turned to her mother with a

smile. "Don't worry, Mother," she said. "Everything will be good, with Hashem's help. Only by helping others can I really live in This World—and keep on living in the World to Come. The food will have to wait a little longer; there's just so much to be done! But don't worry—I'm not hungry."

She ate enough bread to *bentch*, and left to help the two women.

• • •

Once, a fashionably dressed young man ran into Sarah Schenirer's classroom, tears pouring down his cheeks. The girls were surprised. Obviously he had come to ask for their teacher's help, but he didn't look like he needed money. What could he want?

"Frau Schenirer," he said, "my child is very sick. The doctors have already given up on him. Only Hashem can help him recover. Please," he begged, "come with me to *daven* at the grave of the Rema. Plead with Hashem to heal my son."

Instantly understanding how critical her *tefillos* could be, Frau Schenirer excused herself to go *daven* for the sick boy. As she left, she called out to the class, "Pray with me for the recovery of this child!"

• • •

Sarah Schenirer would do anything to help a person in need. If she couldn't raise the money that someone needed, she would sign a paper that allowed him to borrow money, which she would then have to pay back if he couldn't. When that, too, was impossible, she would not rest until she found some other way to get the funds that were needed.

Before each holiday, Sarah Schenirer worked twice as hard to help people. She really wanted everyone to be able to celebrate Yom Tov with joy. Up until Erev Yom Tov, she would be distributing funds. The older girls were a big help with this. On Purim they carried beautiful *mishloach manos*, with all types of delicacies, to the homes of the poor.

Because she did so much walking, there was a time when Sarah Schenirer's shoes began to fall apart. With winter coming, she could no longer put off buying a new pair. She began to save up money for this, keeping the specially designated coins and bills in a drawer in her desk. One day, a poor woman knocked on Sarah Schenirer's door. The woman said that her daughter was sick but that she had no money to buy medicine for her. Sarah Schenirer had no *tzedakah* money to give the woman, but she did have her shoe money. Without hesitation, she reached for it and gave it to the woman.

My shoes can wait, she thought. *But medicine is a matter of life and death.*

When Sarah Schenirer's family found out what she had done, they were very upset. "You were supposed to buy shoes with that money!" they said to her. "You need to protect your feet!"

"I did buy protection for my feet—protection that will last forever!" she answered serenely.

CHAPTER NINE

Bais Yaakov Spreads

Sarah Schenirer worked hard teaching her students, now numbering in the eighties. Meanwhile, her mind was working nonstop.

I'm so glad to be helping the girls of Cracow, she thought. *But how can I help the girls in other cities, too? It isn't right for them to be deprived of a Jewish education just because they don't live in Cracow. I really want to help them, as well. But how? I need to be here. I can't be everywhere at the same time!*

One day, a wonderful idea came to her: *I know! I'll ask my two best and oldest students to help! I'll train them to be teachers, and have them take over for me here while I go and set up schools for the girls*

of other cities. With a few weeks of intense training, I'm sure they can do it!

A new era began. Sarah Schenirer left her school in the hands of her two most trusted students. Then she boarded a train and began her travels. She visited many different villages, speaking in each one about the need to teach girls Torah. She told the mothers all about her school in Cracow.

"You spend so much on your daughters—on food and clothes and everything that they need. But your main goal is to raise them to be devoted Jews; how can you expect that to happen if you don't give them spiritual food, as well? Let's start a Bais Yaakov school here, like the one in Cracow. It's the only way to save your girls!"

Again and again, she repeated the same words. In a number of towns, she was welcomed by the *rabbanim*, who had heard of her good work. When she came to Gur, the Gerrer Rebbe's sister told him about what Sarah Schenirer was doing.

"Of course we must do what we can to teach our girls!" the Rebbe exclaimed. "They have been neglected until now." He gave Frau Schenirer his warm blessings and encouragement.

But in most places, there were many people who were against what she was trying to do. Some of them said, "You're old-fashioned! Now is a new time, when Jews can be just like the non-Jews. We can be both Jewish *and* secular! Why are you trying to put a stop to this?"

Sarah Schenirer had been called "old-fashioned" many times before, and just as it hadn't bothered her back when she was a girl, it didn't bother her now. She simply answered, "There are always new times, but Hashem commanded us to be His People during *all* times. And no, we can't be both Jewish and secular. We have seen that it doesn't work!"

With Hashem's help, Sarah Schenirer was very successful on her travels. By the time she returned to Cracow, there were messages waiting for her from

many towns. "Send us teachers! Everything is ready for them. We want to start a Bais Yaakov of our own! Please help us, so we can stop losing our daughters!"

The time had come for the Bais Yaakov movement to spread.

Sarah Schenirer was very happy, and she thanked Hashem for helping her. She knew she was at an important point in history. She had to work quickly and send teachers to start the new Bais Yaakov schools, but what teachers could she send? Could she send her own students to be the teachers?

The girls are still so young! she thought. *But… they are overflowing with all the wonderful Torah which they have been taught here. I think they are ready for the responsibility of teaching others.*

The town of Radom was first on Sarah Schenirer's list. There were many girls there, girls who were begging for a teacher so they could learn Torah.

Immediately Frau Schenirer thought of her student Gittel.

I will send Gittel to be the teacher in Radom! She's very young, but she's full of a love for Torah. I'm sure she'll do a wonderful job.

Sarah Schenirer went with Gittel on the train to Radom. She helped Gittel write her first speech that she would give to the women and girls of the town. Gittel had never given a speech before. She was very nervous. Sarah Schenirer was also nervous.

Gittel is a wonderful girl—but she really is so young! Will the women of Radom be able to respect a girl of her age? Will the girls be able to respect a teacher who isn't much older than they are? What if they all laugh at her? And can Gittel even think of herself as a teacher? She's just a young girl in braids!

Frau Schenirer reached deep inside her bag. She found some hairpins and used them to fix Gittel's hair into a knot at the back of her head.

"Yes! That helps," Sarah said, lovingly patting the last hairs into place on Gittel's head. "It makes you look older."

Racheli David

"But young ladies wear their dresses a bit longer," Gittel pointed out hesitantly.

"Well, that's no problem," Sarah Schenirer said. "Remember that before I was a teacher, I was a seamstress!"

Gittel stood very still as Sarah Schenirer let down the hem of her dress.

"Yes! That looks even better," Frau Schenirer said approvingly. "You look much older now! Come, let's say some Tehillim and *daven*. Hashem will surely help you succeed."

In Radom, Sarah Schenirer and Gittel saw huge posters on the walls, announcing their arrival. All the ladies came to hear the speeches. They were curious to see Frau Schenirer and the new teacher.

Sarah Schenirer spoke first, and then it was Gittel's turn. She cleared her throat and slowly began. She turned to look at her beloved teacher. How pleased Sarah Schenirer looked. Knowing that Hashem and her teacher were with her, Gittel no

longer felt afraid at all. Her voice grew stronger and calmer. She had such dignity that no one thought of her as just a young girl. Everyone was paying careful attention to her powerful words.

When Gittel finished her speech, Sarah Schenirer hugged her. With eyes filled with joyful tears, she turned to the audience.

"Mothers of Radom! Would you like this young lady to open a Bais Yaakov school here in your town?" she asked.

"Yes! Yes!" all the women answered. "We want our daughters to grow up to be Bais Yaakov girls—just like her! We promise to send them to the school, and we will find the money to pay for the school!"

Sarah saw that, with Hashem's help, the new Bais Yaakov of Radom was on its way. It was now time for her to move on to the next town…and then the next one…and the next…

Sarah Schenirer found traveling difficult. It was hard to spend so much time away from home,

away from her students, and away from her family. Despite the hardships, Sarah Schenirer took many students to one town after another, setting them up as Bais Yaakov teachers. She did not leave the towns until her students, the new teachers there, were settled, and the new Bais Yaakov schools had been established.

Before she left, she gave her students lots of encouragement. She knew how much strength they would need in order to stand up to the pressure of those who would try to destroy what they would build.

"Remain proud Jewish women," she told her precious students. "Remind yourself again and again that you are a favored daughter of the King of kings. If you keep this idea in the forefront of your mind, it will help you succeed."

CHAPTER TEN

Standing Strong in Difficult Situations

Sarah Schenirer never seemed to slow down. Maybe that was because her heart and soul poured energy into everything she was doing. Things didn't always go smoothly for her, but Sarah Schenirer's strong faith kept her going.

One day Sarah Schenirer was supposed to catch a train to southern Germany for an important meeting with people interested in helping Bais Yaakov. She mistakenly boarded the wrong train and ended up in Frankfurt. *There must be a reason why Hashem brought me here*, she thought.

She was directed to a kosher hotel, where she was received by the owner's daughter. The young

woman introduced herself. "My name is Hansi Gross."

"My name is Sarah Schenirer. I'm from Cracow."

"Do I have the merit to meet the famous Sarah Schenirer?" Hansi asked in amazement.

The two became fast friends, and Hansi went on to found Bais Yaakov schools in Germany and Czechoslovakia, and in later years, in Eretz Yisrael. All due to the "wrong" train Sarah Schenirer took!

• • •

When Sarah Schenirer traveled with her student Zelda to the town of Sakrovitz, she saw that there were many troublemakers in the opening class. Frau Schenirer knew that she couldn't leave Zelda alone to deal with them. She invited the girls to her room and spoke to them all night long, until she had won them over and they were eager to become true Bais Yaakov girls.

• • •

As mentioned before, many people were very against what Sarah Schenirer was doing, especially at the beginning. Still, she always saw the good in everything—even in these kinds of difficulties.

Once, someone threw a rock at one of her young students. Sarah Schenirer picked up the rock. She held it high and said, “This is not the only stone that will be thrown at us. There will be many more. We will use these stones to build a beautiful Bais Yaakov school in this city!” And that is what she did.

• • •

Sarah Schenirer taught her students that whenever they met up with hardship, they should look for the light that Hashem had surely hidden inside the darkness. She would remind them that, “A little light drives away much darkness.”

Sometimes the towns and villages had no money to pay the new teachers. Sometimes the teachers did not have a nice place to live or teach. But the

dedicated students of Sarah Schenirer were not worried about money or comfort. They only wanted to be like her and teach more Jewish girls.

In some of the schools, there were girls whose parents were not as *Torahdik* as they should have been. These children had a hard time at home.

On one visit to a Bais Yaakov school in a small village, Sarah Schenirer asked the children, "Who is doing the mitzvah of *kibbud av v'eim*, honoring your parents? Whoever is doing this mitzvah—please stand up!"

All the girls stood up—except for one girl, who burst into tears.

"My father gets angry at me for spending so much time studying my lessons and for being so careful about mitzvos," she sobbed. "It's hard for me to honor him and listen to him." Raising her tear-filled eyes to Frau Schenirer, she asked, "What am I supposed to do?"

Sarah Schenirer hugged the girl and kissed her forehead. "But you *are* keeping the mitzvah of *kibbud*

av, for you listen to your Father in Heaven!" she said. "You honor Him and listen to what He wants you to do. Stand up, my child, stand up."

• • •

Although Sarah Schenirer never had children of her own, she loved her students as only a mother could, and they loved her back with their whole heart. Her students often described her "*azoi vi a gutte Mamme*—like a wonderful mother." Certainly, it was because she was such an encouraging and loving presence, so full of warmth and praise, among her other wonderful attributes.

When the first of her students married and had a child, Sarah Schenirer came to wish the new mother mazel tov and to bless the newborn baby. Her excitement was obvious.

"This is my first grandchild!" she declared, her face shining, her eyes filled with joy.

• • •

Sarah Schenirer never wanted anything for herself. She always insisted, "I have everything I need." She cared only about others and what they might need. For years, her students tried to persuade her to accept a Persian fur coat as a gift. She could have benefited greatly from such a warm coat, given all of the traveling she did for Bais Yaakov. She would go from city to city, and from town to town, often in open carriages and in the freezing cold of the Polish winters. But when the fur coat was offered to her, Sarah Schenirer simply smiled and shook her head.

"I'm not cold. The thought of visiting Bais Yaakov students and their brave, devoted teachers makes me warm."

Her students were concerned about her. Just the idea of Frau Schenirer traveling so many days, in such freezing temperatures, made them shiver! One day the girls came up with an idea they hoped would convince their beloved teacher to accept the coat.

"Frau Schenirer, you collect money for *tzedakah*. You have to look presentable. It makes a difference in the amount of money people will give you."

At long last, Sarah Schenirer was convinced. Her response: "*Far Zein liben Numen*...to glorify Hashem's Name, I will even wear a Persian fur coat if I have to." And she did.

CHAPTER ELEVEN

Her Students Always on Her Mind

From 1921 to 1924, Sarah Schenirer started over fifty Bais Yaakov schools, where thousands of Jewish girls studied. It was an enormous amount of work for her, but a work of love and joy. Sarah Schenirer understood that each new school meant more girls who would be living as exemplary *bnos Yisrael.*

Many of her students were forced to leave school early to help support their families. Sarah Schenirer was concerned about these fourteen- and fifteen-year-old girls, who were entering a world outside the shelter of Bais Yaakov. She knew that she must protect them.

She did two things. First, she tried helping these girls find jobs in places where it would be easier for them to stay *frum*, and she taught them skills that would allow them to work at home. The girls learned how to make dresses, men's shirts, women's hats, and more.

Sarah Schenirer knew that if a person doesn't learn and grow, his *yetzer hara* will surely lead him to sin. To make sure that didn't happen to her working girls, Sarah Schenirer did the second thing: with the help of the Agudah, she founded an organization called Bnos Agudas Yisrael. Bnos offered activities such as *shiurim* and *chessed* projects during the evenings. It was something exciting that working girls could do together with friends. Sarah saw it as another way of making sure that the life of the Jewish girl was rich with joy and meaning.

Bnos programs usually began at 7:00 p.m. and ended at 10:00 p.m. One *shiur* followed another, on various topics. Sometimes the program included

fun activities. Bnos also offered various committees that girls could join. Some took care of *bikur cholim*; others collected pieces of challah and slices of cake and distributed them to the needy for Shabbos. Another committee was responsible for preparing the monthly Rosh Chodesh event for the girls, a very exciting evening which everyone looked forward to.

• • •

Sarah Schenirer continued to take an interest in her students' lives even when they were no longer in her school. One day she knocked on the door of Reb Binyamin Zussman, the man who helped her with many of her activities. Without sitting down, she explained why she had come. "I know that your family is close with Gittel N. I noticed that she has become friendly with girls who are taking her to bad places. Something must be done immediately. I am certain that you will come up with a way to help her." Before she turned to leave, she added, "I am counting on you, Reb Binyamin."

Indeed, Reb Binyamin was able to convince Gittel to fill her life with positive activities. She eventually became an exemplary wife and mother, a woman who was able to help and encourage others—all thanks to Sarah Schenirer's sharp eyes and warm heart.

• • •

When something needed to be done, Sarah Schenirer acted immediately. One morning she appeared at Reb Binyamin's house, looking for an old issue of the magazine *Kinder Garten.* "It had a marvelous article about Shabbos Hagadol. I couldn't get it out of my mind. I am certain the girls will enjoy it as much as I did. I would like to copy and distribute it to all the Bais Yaakov schools. Do you think you might have a copy?"

The issue she was looking for was quickly located. Sarah Schenirer was thrilled. "Thank you so much, Reb Binyamin! Now I can go home and eat my breakfast."

• • •

How did Sarah Schenirer have the time to do so much? She was very careful with her time. She would often repeat the words of Dovid Hamelech, "*Limnos yameinu kein hoda*—Teach us to count our days" (*Tehillim* 90:12), which refers to making sure each moment of our lives is used to its fullest.

She made it her business to be punctual, and she encouraged her students to do the same. If a speech was supposed to be given at 8:00, she made sure to be there on time, even if everyone told her that it would probably not start until much later.

"It's amazing how much you can do if you don't waste time!" she would tell her students.

And indeed, with her time she did a lot more than most people could do. In the beginning, the Bais Yaakov schools had no books for the girls to study from—so she wrote her own books for them. When her girls became teachers, she would sit up all night, after a full day of teaching, writing lesson plans

and lectures on every subject in the curriculum. These precious notebooks were the text used by all of her teachers, even decades later, when they were respected leaders of their own schools.

Once, Chanah G., a student of Sarah Schenirer, caught a glimpse of her beloved teacher at 4:00 a.m. She was sitting in the midst of piles of papers. In her hand was a pencil on which she rested her forehead, eyes closed. After about ten minutes, she lifted her head and glanced at her watch.

"*Oy vey!*" she exclaimed. "I slept for ten minutes, and I have so much to do!"

A half hour later, Chanah saw Sarah Schenirer enter the room where the girls were sleeping. She walked from bed to bed, picking up fallen blankets and untangling jumbles of sheets as she lovingly made sure that each girl was properly covered.

• • •

Once the schools were set up, Sarah Schenirer would visit each of them. The children loved the

visits and looked forward to the next one. Sarah Schenirer would ask the girls questions, compliment their answers, and applaud their achievements. She spent time helping the teachers with their problems and giving them new teaching materials she had prepared.

Before Sarah Schenirer arrived at her girls' schools, the teachers would inform their students what a special woman she was. They would prepare an entire program in her honor, with Yiddish songs and even a poem composed especially for her. By the time the great day arrived, everyone would be shivering with excitement.

On one visit to a Bais Yaakov far away, Sarah Schenirer was met at the train station by the students and their teacher. Each of the girls wanted the privilege of personally greeting Frau Schenirer. Sensing each girl's excitement, Sarah Schenirer made sure to have a smile and a kind word for every one of them.

The teacher had a horse and buggy waiting to take Sarah Schenirer into the village. The students were not happy about being unable to escort their honored visitor themselves, by foot. Two of the more strong-minded girls were determined not to leave her. They grabbed hold of the back of the buggy's frame and held tight.

Their teacher was so embarrassed. She scolded the two and ordered them to jump down from the buggy. Sarah Schenirer gently informed her dear student, the children's teacher, "Children should not be distanced when they wish to come close. They should not be forced down when they are trying to ascend."

Sarah Schenirer got off the buggy and linked arms with her two admirers. Smiling, she said, "I'll walk with you. You lead—I will follow."

The girls were overjoyed. As for their young teacher, Sarah Schenirer's valuable lesson would accompany her forever.

• • •

In the town of Chrzanow, a stunning reception was prepared for Sarah Schenirer's visit. She was ushered into a beautifully decorated auditorium, where the table was set with all kinds of fruits and other delicacies.

The girls crowded around, waiting for her to sit down and taste the wonderful foods they had prepared. Sarah Schenirer, though, was fully focused on the children themselves.

"What's your name?" she asked one of the girls.

"Chanah," was the reply.

"Chanah'le, come here and tell me what *brachah* you make on this fruit and on this cookie."

Chanah answered correctly. Sarah Schenirer's face lit up with joy. She praised the girl and blessed her.

Then she turned to one of the older girls and asked, "What did you learn today?"

"We learned all about *tzedakah* and *chessed*," the girl answered.

Sarah Schenirer was pleased. “Tell me, girls, what kind of *chessed* did you do this week?”

Hands were raised eagerly.

“I made an extra sandwich for a girl who was coming to school without lunch,” said one student.

“We collect prepared meals from families and deliver them to Jewish patients in hospitals,” said another student.

“Girls, I am so proud of your *chessed* activities,” Sarah Schenirer declared with an encouraging smile. “I see that you understand the importance of *tzedakah* and *chessed*. Dear children,” she continued with motherly love, “I want you to remember how important it is to pay attention to what other people need and to help them to the best of your ability.”

Before she left, she blessed the girls. “May Hashem enable you to continue making progress in your studies and acquire more and more *yiras Shamayim*.”

• • •

Sarah Schenirer's former students, who were now teachers, were eager to have their teacher share in the joy of their accomplishments. They would often invite her for special occasions. Sarah Schenirer never refused an invitation. It was an opportunity to show her support for her teachers who worked so hard.

At the end of the school year, Sarah Schenirer visited a certain Bais Yaakov to participate in the final oral exams. Sarah Schenirer beamed with joy as the children confidently responded to one question after another.

As soon as the last question was answered, Sarah Schenirer drew the girls into a celebratory dance. While they danced, they sang, "*V'taher libeinu*," which asks Hashem to purify our hearts.

Sarah Schenirer had the ability to turn every situation into a learning opportunity. When they'd finished their dance, Sarah Schenirer turned to the

וטהר ליבנו
לעבדך באמת...

girls and asked, "What is the best way to acquire a pure heart?"

"By having a good heart," one girl replied.

"By having fear of G-d," was the next answer.

A third felt that good character would get you there. Someone else was convinced that compassion was the way to go.

Sarah Schenirer turned to the youngest in the group. "What do you think?" she asked her.

The girl blushed to the roots of her hair as she softly replied, "I don't know."

Pulling the girl close for a hug, Sarah Schenirer called out with delight, "You are right! A girl who is ready to admit that she does not know is always ready to listen and to learn. This is the kind of person who will eventually acquire a pure heart!"

• • •

When the Bais Yaakov of Bendin completed *Sefer Bereishis*, they wanted to celebrate with a play

called *Yaakov and Eisav*. Without hesitation, Sarah Schenirer traveled to Bendin to see the girls perform. As she sat there in the audience, it was clear to all how much Frau Schenirer was enjoying herself. She was moved by the sad parts and laughed heartily at the funny scenes.

• • •

Although she spent much of her time on the road, Sarah Schenirer never complained. She would arrive back in Cracow, her shoes dusty and her clothes wrinkled, and nevertheless, she would hurry straight from the train station to class or to join in the activities of her Bnos girls, without even stopping at home first. The girls could see how hard it was for her to keep her eyes open, but she would not miss an opportunity to see her dear children and share with them some words of encouragement.

CHAPTER TWELVE

The Bais Yaakov Teachers' Seminary

Sarah Schenirer was very happy to see how many students were filling the Bais Yaakov schools. By 1924, Sarah Schenirer's first Bais Yaakov school, in Cracow, had 280 students—with many more attending the new schools all over Poland. Meanwhile, in Sarah Schenirer's home, she had started a teachers' training seminary, with twenty-five girls, ages fifteen and sixteen, living and studying with her, training to become teachers themselves.

The girls loved the seminary. They called their teacher "Sarah Imeinu—our Mother Sarah." They learned so much from her lessons—and they learned even more from her actions: her *tznius*,

her heartfelt *davening*, her *bitachon*, her *chessed*, her *middos*.

When she said something was forbidden, the girls felt that the deed was something they would never consider doing, and the enthusiasm with which she performed a mitzvah inspired them to follow suit.

• • •

The girls in the seminary went with Sarah Schenirer to shul every Shabbos. One stormy Shabbos morning, the girls stood by the window, watching the hail and snow fall from the sky.

Frau Schenirer came into the room. “Why aren’t you ready to go to shul, girls?” she asked.

“When we saw the bad weather outside, we decided we would *daven* here instead,” the girls explained.

“No, my daughters,” Sarah Schenirer answered gently. “Why should we allow the bad weather to stop

us? You certainly remember the verse in Tehillim, '*B'veis Elokim nehaleich b'ragesh*—To the house of Hashem we went together.' The word *b'ragesh* contains the initial letters of *barad*, *ruach*, *geshem*, and *sheleg*—hail, wind, rain, and snow—which alludes to the fact that we go to shul, Hashem's house, even in these types of weather. So...off we go!" she declared with a smile. And off they went.

• • •

At the Shabbos table, the seminary girls would sing *zemiros* with their teacher, and after singing, Sarah Schenirer would inspire them with stories and meaningful ideas.

One Shabbos night, after the *seudah*, she was so tired, she couldn't move. The girls made a circle and began dancing and singing. Sarah Schenirer forgot how tired she was, and joined the dancing with great enthusiasm.

On Erev Rosh Chodesh, the girls would go together with their teacher to the cemetery, where

they *davened* at the graves of Rav Moshe Isserles, Rav Yoel Sirkes, the Rebbe Rav Heschel of Cracow, and many other tzaddikim.

• • •

During *bedikas chametz* one year, the seminary girls saw that their teacher was exhausted from all of her Pesach preparations. They begged her to rest a while and finish looking for *chametz* later.

Rather than rest, Frau Schenirer told them, “It’s late! Do you think I will be done with tonight’s work after we have finished our search for *chametz*? No, no! After that, I will start checking my heart for *chametz*—which will take so much longer. How can I rest when there is still so much to do?”

• • •

The seminary girls were happy to be living with their beloved teacher, but there was no question that it was very crowded. As for Sarah Schenirer, she wanted so badly for even more girls to attend

her teachers' seminary...but where would she put them? Her home was only so big.

One day, Sarah Schenirer had a visitor, a wealthy man by the name of Reb Asher Spira, who had heard about the seminary and had come to see it with his own eyes. Before leaving, he put a large gold coin on the table.

"Frau Schenirer," he said. "This coin will go toward buying the cornerstone of a large building for your seminary. Hold on to it. I will be back with the rest of the money."

Sarah Schenirer couldn't believe her ears. She wondered if the man would really ever come back, but she took the coin and put it away. "Who knows?" she murmured to herself.

In 1924 there was a major gathering in Warsaw to help Bais Yaakov. Many *rabbanim* came, including the Chafetz Chaim, the Gerrer Rebbe, and Rav Meir Shapiro of Lublin. Many guests from other lands came, too. They joined with respected members of

Racheli

Agudas Yisrael to discuss Bais Yaakov and to praise Sarah Schenirer.

Rav Meir Shapiro, who had visited the Bais Yaakov Seminary, described what he'd seen there. He spoke about the letters pouring in from all over Eastern Europe, from Jewish communities begging for teachers. Then he asked everyone who was there to help him build a real home for the Bais Yaakov Teachers' Seminary in Cracow. Many answered his call and joined hands to help Bais Yaakov reach its goals.

Soon after, Sarah Schenirer received a visit from a familiar-looking man.

"Do you recognize me?" he asked Sarah Schenirer. She did. It was Reb Asher Spira, the man who had given her the gold coin for her seminary.

"I have traveled all over the world collecting money for your school," he said. "Now we are ready to build."

A short time later, the dream that had become so many people's own, was on its way to turning into reality. A beautiful five-story building, with accommodations for 125 students, was slowly rising at 10 Stanislawa Street in Cracow.

The Bais Yaakov Teachers' Seminary now had a home of its own.

CHAPTER THIRTEEN

Sarah Schenirer's Final Days

Sarah Schenirer filled every moment of her life with good deeds, constantly helping and doing things for her students and others. Often, the girls who were having trouble sleeping at night would see the light on in their teacher's room. The light would remain on throughout the night and into the morning, as Frau Schenirer busily wrote letter after letter of encouragement to her students who were teaching all over Poland. Sometimes she would be working on the program for the Teachers' Seminary in Cracow. She also still took a few minutes at night to write down her thoughts in her diary.

Before she went to bed, Sarah Schenirer would think about everything she had done that day. She would thank Hashem for everything He had done for her, and ask Him to keep helping her. She would forgive everyone who may have tried to harm her, and she would ask Hashem to forgive her for whatever she might have done wrong.

The wonder of it all was that no matter how late she went to sleep at night or how tired she was the next day, she always had a smile for everyone. She never lost her temper, never spoke sharply, never complained. She was always up bright and early each morning, ready to greet her girls with a welcoming and happy face.

• • •

Late one night, a student begged Sarah Schenirer to go to sleep. "You have a long day ahead of you tomorrow. You must rest."

"How can I go to sleep?" Sarah Schenirer asked. She was very upset. "When I think about this day's

events, I realize that I have not done any *chessed* today! When we sleep, our *neshamah* goes up to Shamayim and shows Hashem every good thing we did that day. How can I let my *neshamah* stand before Hashem with empty hands?"

"I know someone for whom our dear teacher can do a *chessed* right now," the young girl said.

Sarah Schenirer jumped up from her chair and reached for her coat. "You do? Please tell me who and where this person is! I'm ready!" She forgot how late it was and how tired she was feeling.

"Our dear teacher can do a *chessed* for her students. She can go to sleep so that she will wake up refreshed tomorrow."

Sarah Schenirer smiled. "My dear student, you have given me new life. I will do as you say. Good night."

• • •

For a while, Sarah Schenirer wasn't feeling well, but she didn't tell anyone about it. One day, one of

her young teachers told her that she didn't feel well enough to teach that day; she needed someone else to take over her teaching responsibilities.

Sarah Schenirer answered, "I understand. I never knew what it meant to be ill, but now I do."

Suddenly, her students realized that Sarah Schenirer didn't look so well. Her family and friends insisted that she slow down and take care of herself, but she did not listen...until one Friday evening when, after lighting the Shabbos candles, she collapsed.

Realizing that she would not be able to go to the seminary that night, she burst into tears. Nobody had ever seen her cry like that before.

"Are you in pain?" family members asked, deeply concerned.

"No, it's not physical pain that is making me cry," she replied. "It is the pain of not being able to be with my children and say *Shir Hashirim* with them in my usual way on Erev Shabbos."

Then she remembered: it was Shabbos. The Shabbos Queen must be welcomed with joy! She immediately put a smile on her face, determinedly replacing her worry with faith and trust in Hashem.

Unfortunately, Sarah Schenirer did not get better, and she needed to be hospitalized. When she was admitted to the hospital for an operation, she was sure that all would be well. She confided in her diary what troubled her more than anything else: *For the first time in twenty-three years, I did not* daven *with a* minyan, *and I did not spend Shabbos with my girls.*

When Chanah G., a Bais Yaakov student, came to visit, Frau Schenirer gave her a list of all of her debts that she had to repay. Not one was a personal debt. All of the money she had borrowed was for *tzedakah* purposes. Then, before Chanah left, Frau Schenirer reminded her that Hashem must be served with joy.

Sarah Schenirer never recovered from her illness. Even after her hospitalization, she kept getting weaker and weaker. Her family and friends decided

to take her to Vienna to consult with doctors there. Sarah Schenirer felt confident that her trip would be a success. Years ago, her *neshamah* had been revived in Vienna; certainly now, Hashem would heal her body there.

Her letters from Vienna were full of encouragement for her dear children. Her only request was that they *daven* for her to have a *refuah sheleimah*. Countless chapters of Tehillim were said on behalf of Sarah bas Roiza.

Unfortunately, Sarah Schenirer came back from Vienna too weak to leave her bed. Her closest students gathered around her. When they saw how weak she was, they could barely hold back their tears.

It was clear that Sarah Schenirer did not have much time left in This World. She slept a lot, but whenever she opened her eyes and saw a student at her side, she would murmur, "I feel so much better in the presence of my daughters."

Racheli David

It was Erev Shabbos, the 26th of Adar I, 5695 (March 1, 1935). Frau Schenirer asked one of her beloved students to set up her candlesticks near her bed, and she lit her candles early. Ignoring the terrible pain she was in, Sarah Schenirer gave her students her last instructions. She asked that her students be true to everything she had taught them, and after that, she left This World.

• • •

Sarah Schenirer's work continued to blossom even after her passing. Just a few years later, there were 250 Bais Yaakov schools, with some *40,000* students. These schools were not only in Poland but also in Hungary, Austria, Czechoslovakia, Romania, Lithuania, and Eretz Yisrael. From these Bais Yaakov schools came forth a new generation of women who embraced Torah and mitzvos with pride.

Sarah Schenirer thought she was training her "daughters" for the test of living as good Jewish

wives and mothers. But instead, they were to face a very different test. Not long after her *petirah*, World War II broke out. Many Bais Yaakov students were sent to concentration camps. There are numerous stories of their *mesirus nefesh* during the war, how these girls held on to their *emunah* and how they performed *chessed* even in the darkest of times, continuing to uphold the lessons Frau Schenirer had taught them. Most of these girls died *al kiddush Hashem.*

But some lived—and went on to build Bais Yaakov schools in the United States, in Eretz Yisrael, and in many other countries. Whenever these women had to make a decision about how to run their schools, they would ask themselves, "What would my teacher say? What would Sarah Schenirer tell me if she were here right now?"

Today, tens of thousands of girls go to Bais Yaakov schools. In a way, each Bais Yaakov student is like another daughter of Sarah Schenirer's. Her

magnificent legacy continues on as we walk proudly in the path she set out for us, doing all that we can to bring *nachas* to Hashem.

EPILOGUE

The Legendary Students of Sarah Schenirer in America

Rebbetzin Vichna Kaplan was born in the city of Slonim in 1913. Vichna was an orphan; by the time she was eleven, she had lost both of her parents. She was brought up by her uncle, the *gaon* and tzaddik Rav Yisrael Yaakov Lubchansky, the *mashgiach* of the Baranowitz Yeshivah. At sixteen she became the prized pupil of Sarah Schenirer. A couple of years later, Vichna became a beloved teacher in the city of Brisk.

In 1937 she came to America to marry Reb Boruch Kaplan. Neither Vichna nor her *chassan* had money.

They got married in Yeshiva Torah Vodaath, with a wedding meal consisting of salami sandwiches, and settled in an apartment in the Williamsburg section of New York. The following year, Vichna started the first Bais Yaakov in America, with all of seven girls. It was an uphill battle. She had to convince American parents that Jewish schools for girls were as important as *yeshivos* for boys.

The first class met around Rebbetzin Kaplan's table. The girls came to Rebbetzin Kaplan's house at 7 o'clock in the evening, four nights a week. They arrived after a day spent in public high school, followed by an afternoon job. These girls didn't want to be there, at least not at first. They had shown up simply because their parents, recognizing the importance of what Rebbetzin Kaplan was trying to do, told them to go.

Rebbetzin Kaplan had a difficult job ahead of her with these Americanized girls, but she was determined to make it work. She took the fire that

Sarah Schenirer had ignited inside of her back in Europe, and brought it to America.

With much *siyata d'Shmaya*, Rebbetzin Kaplan was very successful. She was an incredible teacher. When she taught, her words came from the depths of her soul. She knew how to be strict, how to stand up for what was right, but her firmness was always shown in a quiet, soft way. And she believed in her students, seeing only the good in them.

Her students responded to her in kind. They appreciated her sincerity and goodness, and they didn't want to disappoint her. Slowly but surely, under Rebbetzin Kaplan's care, there began to emerge true Bais Yaakov girls in America.

• • •

Rebbetzin Chava (Weinberg) Pinkus was the first teacher Rebbetzin Kaplan hired for her Bais Yaakov. Chava was an American, yet as a young teenager she had traveled to Cracow to learn in Sarah

Schenirer's seminary. She was Frau Schenirer's only American student.

When Chava first met Sarah Schenirer, she was left speechless by the fiery light that shone from her face. Chava was not offended when Sarah Schenirer immediately, but so lovingly, turned to fix her neckline with a pin. What was considered kosher in America was not up to Sarah Schenirer's halachic standards.

Years later, Chava would tell her daughter, "When Frau Schenirer pinned up my neckline, I felt like she was pinning a medal on me!"

In the beginning, it was hard for Chava to follow the classes. They were given in German and Galician Yiddish, which is very different from the Lithuanian Yiddish that Chava knew, but in a short time she had mastered the language and was doing very well. Although she had only planned to study at the seminary for a year, she ended up staying two whole years.

When many years later, Rebbetzin Chava Pinkus became a teacher in America's first Bais Yaakov, she immediately won over her students with her vivacious personality and her inspiring delivery of ideas.

• • •

Rebbetzin Basya Bender and **Rebbetzin Chava Wachtfogel,** also originally students of Sarah Schenirer, were the next teachers hired by Rebbetzin Kaplan. Rebbetzin Bender was down-to-earth and very knowledgeable in numerous areas. There was a warm glow in her soft, brown eyes. Rebbetzin Wachtfogel's *yiras Shamayim* was transmitted through the *pesukim* she taught and the values she modeled. Her sweet, loving smile lit up her thoughtful face.

• • •

In 1944 Bais Yaakov became a full-fledged high school. Situated in Williamsburg, the school catered to all kinds of girls: *Litvishe*, *Chassidish*, daughters

of *rebbes* and *roshei yeshivah*, and some girls who weren't even *shomer Shabbos*. Rebbetzin Kaplan welcomed anyone who wanted to learn about *Yiddishkeit*.

In 1958 a Boro Park branch of Bais Yaakov was opened, which eventually replaced the original Bais Yaakov in Williamsburg.

Other teachers who taught in Rebbetzin Kaplan's Bais Yaakov were Rebbetzin Rochel Czinner, Rebbetzin Rivka Springer, Rebbetzin Chana Rotenberg, Rebbetzin Shifra Yudasin, Rebbetzin Batsheva Hutner, and Rebbetzin Leah Goldstein. All of them had been students of Sarah Schenirer back in Europe. Working together, these dedicated teachers succeeded in transmitting the Torah values they had acquired in pre-war Europe to their American-born *talmidos*.

In turn, their students went on to found other Bais Yaakov schools, thus continuing the exalted legacy of Sarah Schenirer.

I am one of those students, and you, too, are still being nourished by Sarah Schenirer's original blaze. When you get older *b'ezras Hashem*, it will be up to you to pass the flame on to the next generation.

May all the flames ignited by Bais Yaakov teachers and students of so many generations light the way for the arrival of Mashiach, soon and in our days.

Appendix

There were five *pesukim* from Tehillim that Sarah Schenirer repeated constantly. In one of her final letters, she asked that these *pesukim* always accompany her students throughout their lives. We, too, should constantly remember them:

"*Ivdu es Hashem b'simchah*—Serve Hashem with joy" (*Tehillim* 100:2).

"*Shivisi Hashem l'negdi samid*—I have placed Hashem in front of me always" (*Tehillim* 16:8).

"*Reishis chachmah yiras Hashem*—The beginning of all wisdom is fear of Hashem" (*Tehillim* 111:10).

"*Limnos yameinu kein hoda*—Teach us to count our days" (*Tehillim* 90:12).

"*Toras Hashem temimah meshivas nafesh*—The teachings of Hashem are perfect, renewing life" (*Tehillim* 19:8).